CONTENTS

TEACH YOURSELF TO PLAY THE FOLK HARP

First Book in a Series by

SYLVIA WOODS

All pieces arranged by Sylvia Woods

DEDICATION

This book is dedicated to everyone who uses it to learn to play the folk harp, and to those whose lives will be enriched and enlivened by their music.

THANKS TO:

Katharine, Shawna, and Heidi for being great guinea pigs . . .
Chris and Teresa for their contributions . . .
Janet, Dwight, and Dinah for their photos . . .
Robin for his knowledge and suggestions . . .
Conway and Marjorie for their special assistance . . .
Don for his time and expertise . . .
Lou Ann for her encouragement . . .
and Tommy for his patience, help, and love.

Photos on cover and page 35 by Janet Williamson
Text photos by Dwight Caswell

8th Edition Printing 1992

Woods Music & Books, Inc.
P.O. Box 816, Montrose, CA 91021 USA

ISBN 0-9602990-3-3

INTRODUCTION

Many people feel drawn to the magical and spiritual qualities of the harp, which has come to us through the mists of time. In my travels around the world playing the Celtic harp, I have observed an exciting resurgence of interest in folk harps. A growing number of craftsmen are making harps, and more and more people are learning to play them. Everywhere I have performed, people have approached me asking for information on where to obtain harps and how to play them. I enjoy being able to help people realize their dreams of becoming harpers; that is why I have written this book.

You don't need a teacher or any previous musical training to learn to play the harp (although either of these will be helpful). This book will teach you what you need to know. Each lesson is a bit more advanced than the previous one. Every once in a while the pieces will seem to be a lot harder than the ones before. Try not to let this discourage you. Look on the more difficult pieces as challenges that will help expand your abilities. Pieces like Scarborough Fair, Trip to Sligo, and Shenandoah are not easy to master; but once you do, you will have accomplished a great deal!

This book teaches you the basics of folk harp playing. Once you've completed this book you have a wide selection of music to try. For example, I have written books of Christmas music, Irish music, church music, wedding music, O'Carolan music, and more, all arranged for the folk harp. Write to me at the address below and I'll send you a free catalog.

Please write to me and let me know how you are doing. I like to hear from harpers who are using this book, so I can give any assistance. Also, if you would like help in finding a good harp, I can refer you to several excellent harpmakers who make fine, high-quality instruments.

My harp brings me so much pleasure and a feeling of freedom. I'm sure your harp will do the same for you, and you and your harp will do that for others. With your harp and this book you are off on a great adventure. Enjoy it!

Sylvia Woods

Sylvia Woods
Woods Music & Books, Inc.
P.O. Box 816
Montrose, CA 91021 USA

An audio cassette of Sylvia Woods playing the pieces in this book is available from Woods Music and Books at the address above.

A video of Sylvia Woods giving instruction and helpful hints, as well as showing you how to play the pieces in this book is also available on VHS or Beta format.

PARTS OF A HARP

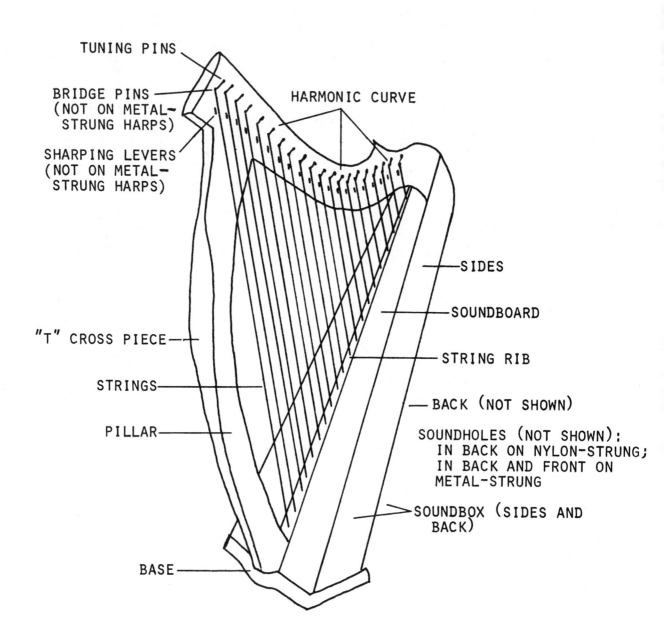

TUNING PINS

BRIDGE PINS
(NOT ON METAL-
STRUNG HARPS)

SHARPING LEVERS
(NOT ON METAL-
STRUNG HARPS)

HARMONIC CURVE

SIDES

SOUNDBOARD

"T" CROSS PIECE

STRING RIB

STRINGS

BACK (NOT SHOWN)

PILLAR

SOUNDHOLES (NOT SHOWN):
    IN BACK ON NYLON-STRUNG;
    IN BACK AND FRONT ON
    METAL-STRUNG

SOUNDBOX (SIDES AND
    BACK)

BASE

BRIEF HISTORY OF THE FOLK HARP

by Christopher Caswell and Robin Williamson

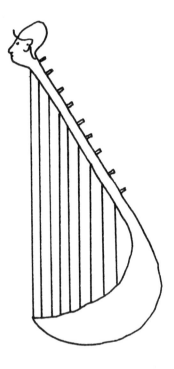

Now that you're learning to play the folk harp, you are carrying on an ancient tradition which has continued for thousands of years. Any culture that had a hunting bow had the fundamental form of a harp, making the harp one of the oldest stringed instruments. These bow harps originated in many areas of the world, and some are still in use today. Carvings, plaques and wall paintings of these harps dating from as early as 3000 B.C. still exist in Egypt and Mesopotamia. Bow harps do not have a pillar (see pg. 6), rather, they are held together by the tension of the strings, themselves.

The first main improvement of the harp was the addition of a rigid pillar, making a triangular frame harp similar to those of today. This harp was probably much easier to tune than the bow harp, and allowed more choice of scales. There is a small statue from the Cyclades (islands near Greece) dated between 3000 and 2000 B.C. which shows a seated man playing what appears to be a frame harp.

In Ireland, the earliest mention of the harp is about 541 B.C., where the harp was made of willow, and the harper's name was Craftiné. The earliest known depiction of a frame harp in the British Isles is on an 8th Century stone cross in Scotland. Here, as well as in other Celtic countries, harpers were very important and well-respected. They were often poets as well as musicians, and were credited with magical powers. Harpers were required to be able to evoke three different emotions in their audience by their music: Geantraighe, or laughter; Goltraighe, or tears; and Suantraighe, or sleep.

The Ancient Celtic harps used in Ireland and Scotland were strung with combinations of brass and steel wire, and possibly silver. The soundboxes were carved from a single piece of wood. In early Wales, they apparently strung some of theirs with horsehair, producing a buzzing sound. Later, they too used brass-strung harps.

Gradually, with the coming of Christianity, the invasions of the Vikings, and social disruption and feuding in the British Isles, the harpers lost much of their influence and power, becoming court minstrels and street musicians.

In the 10th Century, Brian Boru, the Irish hero and warrior king, did much to revive the harp in Ireland, founding the Bardic Order which created a musical heritage and tradition which survived 500 years.

About the time of Brian Boru, Irish harpers were traveling to the highlands of Scotland to study in the harping schools there. By the middle ages, however, the trend had reversed and Scots harpers were commonly traveling to Ireland to learn their craft.

One of the three oldest harps from the British Isles is commonly associated with Brian Boru, although its true history is not known. It is a low-headed lap harp with 30 strings, and is now housed at Trinity College, Dublin. The other two harps are Scottish. The Queen Mary Harp is almost identical to the Trinity College Harp; and the Lamont Harp is slightly larger.

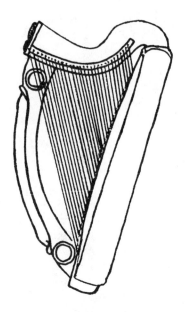

The harp was originally the national instrument of Scotland. Each clan had its own harper who held a position of high esteem. Over centuries of internal feuding among various chieftains, however, the harp was gradually replaced by the more war-like bagpipes. The harp was in full decline in Scotland by the 17th Century.

During the reign of Elizabeth I, the Catholic landowners in Ireland were displaced by Protestant ones. At the same time, the harpers, most of whom were Catholic, fell into disfavor with the government because they supposedly incited rebellion with their songs and music. Once again, the harpers lost status, and many of them fled to Scotland or the continent.

The harps in Europe were gut-strung and generally had narrower, shallower soundboxes built from several pieces of wood. Here, the harp was often used by troubadours as accompaniment for songs in the new fashion of courtly love and chivalry. Traveling Irish harpers met with great response; their louder instruments making a mark on developments which would lead to the pedal harp in about a century.

The Italians produced a triple-strung harp (with three rows of strings) which the Welsh adopted as their national instrument. The Spanish enjoyed double-strung harps, as well as the single-strung harps which they carried with them to the new world.

Towards the end of the 18th Century, the use of the metal-strung or Ancient Celtic harp had died down in Ireland. At a harper's convention in Belfast in 1792, only one player, Denis Hempson, still played in the earlier style with fingernails upon metal strings. The so-called Neo-Celtic harp, which had gut strings, had become more prevalent.

In the early 20th Century, the Celtic revivals in Ireland and Scotland brought new strength to folk harping there, and Neo-Celtic harps were being made in increasing numbers. In the last 20 years, harping has become even more popular in the British Isles and America, and harp building has continued to increase steadily to meet the demand. Within the past 5 years, Ancient Celtic style harps have also been revitalized. The majority of harp making is currently done in the U.S., and the center of folk harp development is the west coast. With more instruments available, use of the folk harp has grown greatly in every field of music.

With your harp, you are contributing to the culture of the future, whose echoes will be heard for centuries to come.

HOLDING THE HARP

There are two basic styles of folk harps: harps held on the lap, and harps that sit on the floor.

To play a <u>lap harp</u>, sit upright in a normal height armless chair (or stool) with your feet flat on the floor. Sit a bit forward on the seat; don't lean against the back of the chair. Put the harp on your lap with the pillar away from you and the soundbox towards your chest. Lean the top of the harp back so that the top of the soundbox rests lightly against your right shoulder. Experiment with the angle of the harp by moving the base closer to your knees, or closer to your body, until you find a position that feels comfortable and secure.

<u>Floor harps</u> can be played by sitting on a low stool. If that is not comfortable, you can sit on a regular height chair and put the harp on a small table. Sit upright and don't lean against the back of the chair. Sit behind the soundbox of the harp (a little to the left) and lean the top towards you so that the soundbox is between your knees. Lightly grip the harp with your knees to help stabilize it. The top of the soundbox rests lightly against your right shoulder. The front of the base of the harp will be off the floor. When the harp is tilted back properly, the strings should be completely vertical, and the harp should be lightly balanced against your shoulder. Experiment with different height stools and how close you are sitting to the harp until you find a comfortable position. You should neither sit too close nor too far away from the harp.

HAND POSITION: NYLON/GUT-STRUNG

The thumb is up higher than the fingers, with the top joint of the thumb inclined a bit towards them; not bent backwards. The hand is slightly cupped, forming a hollow in the palm. The first three fingers are curved in a relaxed manner and contact the strings about 1/4 inch from the tip of the fingers. <u>The little finger is never used, since its reach is not as long as the ring finger</u>. The wrists are in a little towards the strings. The bottom of the hand is turned out a bit so that the hand is not totally parallel to the strings. The fingers should rest lightly on the strings, near the center of each string. Relax the shoulders.

Both elbows should be up so that the forearms are horizontal to the floor. Don't rest them on your legs. When playing the middle or high strings, the right forearm (or wrist for the upper strings) may rest on the side of the soundbox, but should not lean heavily on it. Your arm should be free to move easily up and down the harp. The left arm does not contact the soundbox.

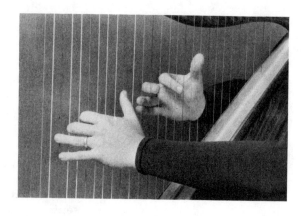

The photos on page 16 show the proper finger action:

Pluck the strings with the finger tips and bring the fingers into the palm of the hand. Use your whole finger in this action; don't just bend the first knuckle. Good sound is produced by using the whole finger and bringing it all the way into the palm. You don't need to worry about the little finger. It should naturally follow the ring finger into the palm.

Pluck the string with the outer edge of the thumb and bring the thumb down until it touches the side of the first finger. Use your whole thumb in this action, not the top joint. Keep the top joint inclined forward a bit; don't let it bend backwards.

The fingernails should be short so they don't hamper the finger action. The nails should never touch the strings.

HAND POSITION: METAL-STRUNG

by Christopher Caswell

The metal-strung, or Ancient Celtic, harps are played for the most part like nylon- or gut-strung harps. There are some notable differences, though.

For the greatest part of their history, metal-strung harps were played with the fingernails. Sometimes they were played with the pads of the fingers for the quieter, softer sound; but their distinctive bell-like voices are best heard when played with the nails.

To play in this fashion, grow the fingernails of the right hand about 1/16th of an inch beyond the fingertips. On the left hand it is only necessary to grow the thumbnail (although all nails can be grown if preferred). This makes it easier to get a balance between the louder low strings and the higher strings, using the thumbnail for brilliance when needed.

Hand position is the same as it is for the nylon-strung, except that the fingers are turned a bit so that the nails reach the strings.

To pluck with the nails, first place the fingertip on the string, as you would for the nylon-strung, and as you pull off, catch the nail on the string. To place your fingers on the strings with the nails only will cause buzzes, and feels very unstable.

Metal strings take less force than nylon strings to set them in motion, so you don't have to pluck very hard to create a big sound. In general, play more lightly on them than you would on a nylon-strung harp.

A great thing about the metal-strung harps is their tremendous after-ring. You can use this to your advantage in simple arrangements. The drawbacks to the long ringing is that clarity can be lost in fast pieces or crowded arrangements. To handle this, you can dampen or muffle the strings just played by placing the fingertips against the strings, or by placing the whole hand flat against the strings, thus stopping them from vibrating.

The playing of metal-strung harps has only recently been revived. It is an area full of experimentation. There are as many styles around as there are players. The above information reflects my own observation, augmented by the findings of friends who have also touched these strings which have been silent too long.

FUNDAMENTALS

We'll begin with some basic definitions:

MUSIC: a. beautiful, pleasing or interesting arrangements of sounds, especially as produced by the voice or instruments
b. written or printed signs for tones

TONE: a sound of definite pitch and duration

PITCH: the degree of highness or lowness of a sound or tone

DURATION: the time during which anything continues

NOTE: a. the written sign to show the pitch and length of a sound, e.g. ♩ ♪ ♪ 𝅝
b. same as tone

Written music is like a map or a diagram of the sounds we hear. The notes are symbols that tell us the pitch and duration of each sound.

Notes are named using the first seven letters of the alphabet: A, B, C, D, E, F, G.

On the harp, all C strings are colored red, and all F strings are blue or black or green. Find one red string on your harp. This is a C. The next higher string in pitch (going up toward the shorter strings on your harp) is a D. The next string is an E. The next is blue or black and is an F. After that is G, A, B and back again to another red C, and so on.

From one string to the next string of the <u>same letter name</u> (i.e. from C to C, or from G to G, etc) is called an <u>octave</u>.

Practice touching various strings on your harp and say their names out loud until you feel certain of them.

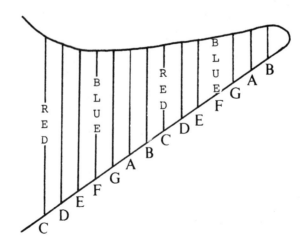

HOW TO READ MUSIC

Notes are written on a set of five lines called a <u>staff</u> or <u>stave</u>:
The placement of notes on the staff tells you the relative pitch
of the tones. In this example, the first note is lower in pitch
than the second note.

<u>Ledger lines</u> are added above or below the staff to increase the
range of the staff.

We do not know the exact pitch of the notes on the staff until we add a <u>clef</u>. A
clef is a symbol which is placed on a staff that indicates what tones the notes
represent.

This is a <u>treble clef</u>: 𝄞 . When it is placed on a staff, these are the names of
the notes on the staff.

To find middle C on your harp, locate the red string that has at least 14 strings
above it and at least 7 strings (preferably 10) below it. For the purposes of
this book, that is middle C.

One way to help you learn which note on the staff corresponds with which letter,
is to make words or phrases out of the letters of the lines and spaces of the
staff. For example:

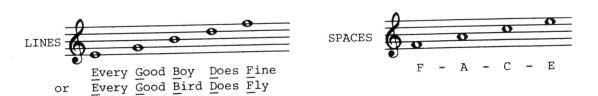

LINES   Every Good Boy Does Fine
    or   Every Good Bird Does Fly

SPACES   F - A - C - E

To help you learn the names of the notes on the staff, go through the pieces in
the first four lessons of this book and name each note. Do this until you feel
certain about the notes and their names.

Each piece of music has a definite beat or pulse. When you clap your hands to a piece, you are clapping to the beats.

Notes ♩ consist of a body ● and a stem │ . These are used to indicate the time value of a note, that is, how many beats it should be held, or its duration.

𝅝 = 4 beats   A <u>whole note</u> has an open body with no stem. It is held 4 beats.

𝅗𝅥 = 2 beats   A <u>half note</u> has an open body and a stem. It is held half as long as a whole note, or 2 beats.

♩ = 1 beat   A <u>quarter</u> note has a filled-in body and a stem. It is held one-quarter as long as a whole note, or 1 beat.

Notes can be written with their stems up or down, it doesn't matter. The pitch of the note is indicated by the position of the body of the note on the staff, not by the stem. For example, these notes are all B's.

Music is divided into units of time called <u>measures</u>. The dividing line between two measures is called a <u>bar line</u>. A <u>double bar</u> indicates the end of a piece or a section of a piece.

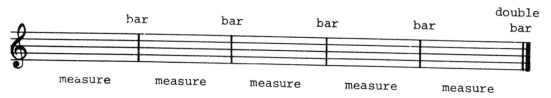

All of the measures in one piece will contain the same number of beats. A <u>time signature</u> (e.g. $\frac{3}{4}$ or $\frac{4}{4}$) will be written at the beginning of a piece to tell you how many beats there are in each measure.

$\frac{3}{4}$ time means that there will be the equivalent of 3 quarter notes, or 3 beats in each measure.

$\frac{4}{4}$ time means that there will be the equivalent of 4 quarter notes, or 4 beats in each measure.

14

When learning a new piece of music, you must be sure that you hold each note the proper number of beats. The best way to ensure this is to count each measure out loud as you play it.

If you are playing in $\frac{4}{4}$ time, you count "1 2 3 4 1 2 3 4 1 2 3 4" etc. evenly at the speed you want to play the piece.

In $\frac{3}{4}$ time, count "1 2 3 1 2 3 1 2 3" etc.

Here are some examples of measures in $\frac{4}{4}$ time and how to count them. In these examples, count "1 2 3 4" in each measure, but only play on the counts circled.

Count "1 2 3 4". Play on all 4 counts since each note gets 1 beat.

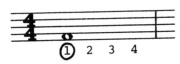

Count "1 2 3 4". Play only on beat 1 since a whole note is held four beats.

Count "1 2 3 4". Play on beat 1 and beat 3 since half notes get two beats each.

Count "1 2 3 4". Play on beat 1 and then on beats 3 and 4.

Count "1 2 3 4". Play on beats 1, 2 and 3.

Here are some examples of measures in $\frac{3}{4}$ time. Count "1 2 3" in each measure, but only play on the circled counts.

Count "1 2 3". Play on all three beats since each note gets one beat.

Count "1 2 3". Play on beats 1 and 3. The first note is held two beats.

Count "1 2 3". Play on beats 1 and 2. The second note is held two beats.

Lesson 1

In this book, the fingers of both hands will be numbered as follows:

Thumb	Index Finger	Middle Finger	Ring Finger
1	2	3	4

Since the little finger is never used, it is not numbered.

❖❖❖

<u>Placing</u> the fingers on the strings before they are needed is an important aspect of harp technique. It provides stability for your fingers and enables you to play more quickly.

A <u>bracket</u> ⌐‾⌐ or ⌐__⌐ is used to indicate fingers that should be placed together. The fingers should be placed on all the notes within the bracket <u>before</u> the first note in the bracket is played.

For example, when playing four ascending notes, such as ⌐C, D, E, F⌐ all four fingers should be placed on their respective strings <u>before</u> playing the first note. Then the strings are plucked one at a time by bringing the fingers into the palm. After all notes in the bracket have been played, the hand should be closed with all fingers in the palm and the thumb resting on top of the second finger.

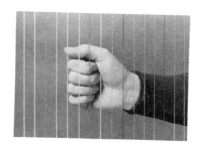

The beginning of Exercise 1 A is played as follows:
  a. place fingers 2 and 1 on the strings
  b. play finger 2
  c. play finger 1
  d. place fingers 2 and 1 on the next strings
  e. play finger 2
  f. play finger 1
  etc.

In Exercise 1 B, three fingers are placed at once; and in Exercise 1 C, all four
fingers are placed together.

Practice these exercises first with the right hand, and then with the left hand an
octave lower. Practice them slowly, being sure that all the fingers in the brackets
are placed before you begin.

EXERCISE 1 A

EXERCISE 1 B

EXERCISE 1 C

At the beginning of each piece in this book is a word indicating the speed at which it should be played. These are the terms I use, in order from the slowest to the fastest.

    very slowly
    slowly
    leisurely
    moderately
    briskly
    fast
    very fast

Also, many pieces have a second word indicating a feeling or emotion (i.e. tenderly, happily, mournfully, etc.). All of these terms are meant only to give a general guideline for the piece.

❖❖❖

When placing the fingers in a bracket, place only the fingers indicated, or you will become confused. That is, if the bracket is └ 4 2 1 ┘, don't place finger 3 on a string. Any finger that is not being used is held near the palm.

❖❖❖

Practice these pieces first with the right hand and then with the left an octave lower. Be sure to count the beats as you play.

Twinkle, Twinkle, Little Star

use Left Hand

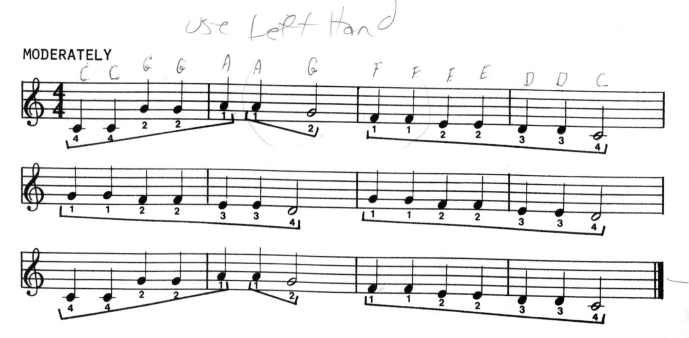

MODERATELY

18

Yankee Doodle

use L H

BRISKLY

Go Tell Aunt Rhodie

L H

MODERATELY

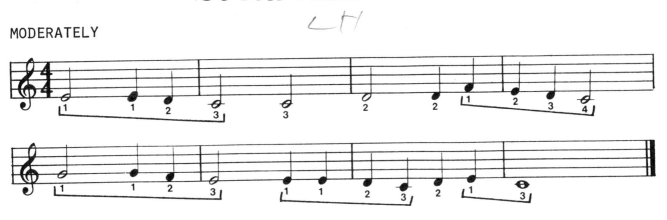

An <u>eighth note</u> has a filled-in body, a stem, and a flag. This is an eighth note ♪
It is held 1/2 beat. Therefore, two eighth notes are equal to one quarter note.
Two or more eighth notes can be grouped together with a line (called a beam)
replacing the flags: ♪ ♪ = ♫   ♪ ♪ ♪ ♪ = ♬

When counting the beats in a measure that contains eighth notes, you still count
"1 2 3 4" as before, but you add the word "and" <u>between</u> each number to create 8
divisions like this: "1 and 2 and 3 and 4 and". Be sure that the basic 1-2-3-4
beat stays the same as it was before. One way to practice this is to clap your
hands in a steady beat and count one number on each clap; then, keeping your
claps steady, add the word "and" between each clap, like this:

clap	clap	clap	clap	clap	clap	clap	clap
1	2	3	4	1 and	2 and	3 and	4 and

19

Here are some examples using eighth notes. In these examples, count " 1 & 2 & 3 & 4 &" in each measure, but only play on the circled counts.

count ①&②&③&④& ①&②&③ & 4 & ①&②&③ & ④& ①&② & ③ & ④&

❖❖❖❖❖❖❖❖❖❖❖❖❖❖❖❖❖❖❖❖❖❖❖❖❖❖❖❖❖❖❖❖❖❖

These pieces have eighth notes in them. Count them very carefully. Practice first with your right hand and then with your left an octave lower.

Lavender's Blue

SLOWLY

❖❖❖❖❖❖❖❖❖❖❖❖❖❖❖❖❖❖❖❖❖❖❖❖❖❖❖❖❖❖❖❖❖❖

Are You Sleeping?

MODERATELY

Lesson 2

This symbol ⌡ is a <u>quarter rest</u>. It gets one beat of silence. When you get to this rest you count one beat, but don't play anything. For example, several measures in The Water is Wide (the next piece) have a rest on the first beat. You still count "1 2 3 4", but do not play anything on beat 1.

Sometimes brackets overlap each other, as in the following exercise. This exercise should be played as follows:

    a. Place all four fingers on the first four notes (C, D, E, F)

    b. Play the first three notes (C, D, E)

    c. Before playing the thumb (keeping it placed), place the 4th finger on the first note of the next measure (D)

    d. Play the thumb, keeping the 4th finger placed

    e. Place the other fingers (3, 2, 1) for the second measure

    f. Repeat from b.

Place 4, 3, 2, 1 | before playing | place 3, | before playing
               1, place 4   2, 1   1 place 4

both hands

Play this exercise first with the <u>right hand</u>, and then with the <u>left hand</u> an octave lower.

EXERCISE 2

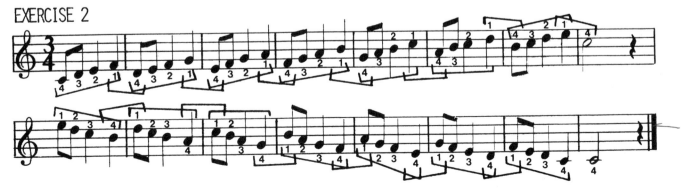

All of the pieces in this lesson should be played first with the right hand and then with the left hand an octave lower.

Remember to place all the fingers within the brackets, but only those that you need.

LH - play Root, 5, 10 (3 octave up), 5 — you can also use 9 instead of 10
quarter notes or eighth notes
ch - (135)

The Water is Wide

VERY SLOWLY

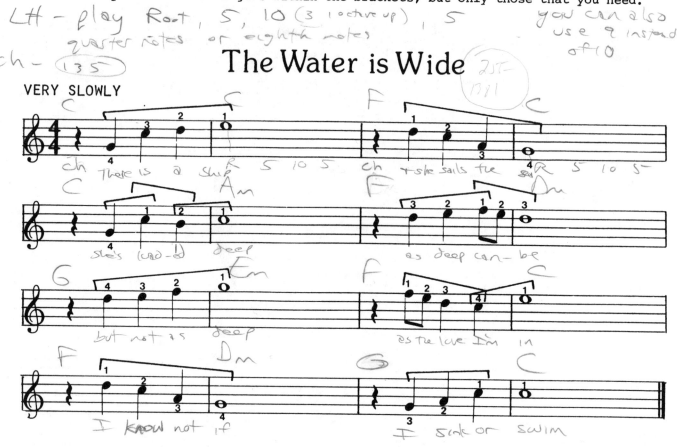

There is a ship ... ch ↑she sails the ...

She's lad-ed deep ... as deep can-be

but not as deep ... as the love I'm in

I know not if ... I sink or swim

White Choral Bells

LEISURELY

Long, Long Ago

Two notes of the same pitch can be <u>tied</u> together like this:
You pluck only the first note, but hold it for the combined
duration of both notes. In this example you play the G only
once, but hold it for 8 full beats. In this next piece,
there are tied notes at the end of the 4th and 8th staves.

SLOWLY

A <u>dot</u> following a note increases the value of the note by <u>one-half of its original value.</u>

♩ = 2 beats   ♩. = 3 beats

♩ = 1 beat   ♩. = 1½ beats

Here are some examples of dotted notes and how to count them. You would play on the circled counts.

count   ① 2 3 ④ ① ② 3 4   ① & 2 ②&③ & ④ &   ① & 2 ②&③ & 4 ④&   ① & 2 ②&③ & 4 &

Country Gardens

Country Gardens was originally a Morris dance tune. A Morris dance is an old English dance performed in costume or disguise. The dancers often wore bells on their legs.

MODERATELY

Allemande

An Allemande is a dance that was popular during the Renaissance.

BRISKLY & COURTLY

T. ARBEAU

Lesson 3

Rests are symbols that indicate periods of silence. There are several kinds of
rests, and each one gets a certain number of beats. Here are the rests and their
time values.

Rests can be dotted, just
like notes. Therefore,

𝄾. = 1½ beats.

4 beats	2 beats	1 beat	½ beat
whole rest	half rest	quarter rest	eighth rest

Throughout the rest of the book, two staves will be joined together. They are
played at the same time. Notes on the top staff are played with the right hand, RH
and notes on the bottom staff are played with the left hand. LH

In this exercise, the left hand plays an octave lower than the written music.
In the other pieces in this lesson, however, the left hand will play as written
(not an octave lower).

EXERCISE 3

Joy To The World

GEORGE F. HANDEL

BRISKLY

Blue Bells of Scotland

The first note of this song is in a measure all by itself, even though it only gets one beat. This is called a "pick-up". When this occurs, the last measure of the song will also have fewer beats than normal. The pick-up plus the last measure will always equal one full measure.

MODERATELY & MARCHLIKE

Minuet

BRISKLY, WITH RESTRAINT

J. S. BACH

Lesson 4

In this lesson you will begin to play with both hands at the same time. Before you start this lesson, go back and play everything in the first three lessons with <u>both hands at the same time</u>. Play the left hand an octave lower than the right. This will help you get used to both hands playing together.

~~~~~~

These are <u>repeat signs</u> ‖: :‖. They indicate that when you get to the second sign, go back to the first sign, repeat that section, then continue. For example:

play measures 1 through 4, repeat 3 and 4, then continue with 5 etc.

If there is only the second sign, then repeat from the beginning. For example:

play measures 1 through 4, repeat 1 through 4, continue with 5 etc.

~~~~~~

EXERCISE 4

This exercise is to get your fingers accustomed to one hand going up while the other goes down. Both hands play at the same time. Repeat it through several times until it flows well. Don't worry if at first your fingers get confused and go the wrong way. This exercise is a bit like trying to pat your head and rub your stomach at the same time. Keep practicing; you'll get it.

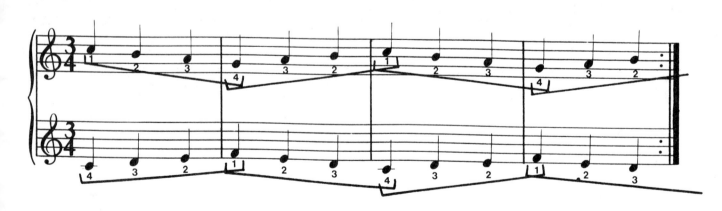

Throughout the rest of this book, practice the right and and the left hand
separately a few times and then learn the piece with both hands together.

All Through the Night

Remember to repeat :‖ the first line of this piece.

VERY SLOWLY, A LULLABY   WALES

In this book I use parentheses (♩) to indicate notes that are part of the melody,
or main tune, but that are played by the left hand rather than the right. I write
the note in both clefs so you can see the continuity of the melody; but the note
in parentheses is not played, as it is duplicated in the left hand.

Robin Adair

or

Eileen Aroon

LEISURELY & SIMPLY

SCOTLAND/IRELAND

Ode to Joy

BEETHOVEN

MODERATELY & MAJESTICALLY

Lesson 5

Most harp music (as well as piano and organ music) is written in two clefs: the treble clef 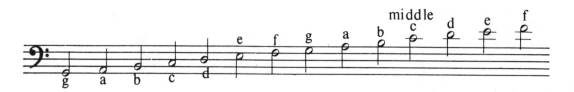, which we have already learned, and the <u>bass clef</u> 𝄢 . Usually, the right hand will play what is written in the treble clef, and the left hand will play what is written in the bass clef. Here are the notes that you will need to know in the bass clef:

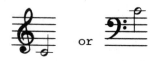

Notice that middle C can be written in either clef: or
These are both the same string.

These other notes can also be written in either clef:

If your harp only has 7 strings below middle C, you will not be able to play the three lowest notes that are used in this book. When these are written in the music, play them an octave higher, as shown here.

To help you learn the bass clef, phrases can be made out of the letters of the notes of the lines and spaces, as we did for the treble clef. For example:

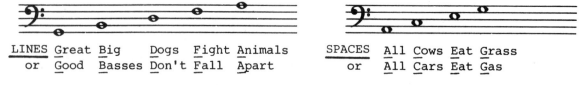

LINES <u>G</u>reat <u>B</u>ig <u>D</u>ogs <u>F</u>ight <u>A</u>nimals
  or   <u>G</u>ood <u>B</u>asses <u>D</u>on't <u>F</u>all <u>A</u>part

SPACES <u>A</u>ll <u>C</u>ows <u>E</u>at <u>G</u>rass
  or   <u>A</u>ll <u>C</u>ars <u>E</u>at <u>G</u>as

Go through some of the pieces in the rest of the book and name the notes in the bass clef. Do this until you feel certain about their names.

In this exercise, place your fingers on the strings one measure ahead. For example, while playing the left hand, place the right hand on the notes in the next measure. Then, while playing your right, place your left, etc. In this manner, try to play the exercise without having to stop at the end of each measure to place.

EXERCISE 5

Drink to Me Only with Thine Eyes

The origin of this tune is unknown, but it is commonly used with the poem by Ben Jonson, written in 1616.

SLOWLY

Planxty George Brabazon

Turlough O'Carolan (1670-1738) is the best known of the Irish harpers. About 200
of his tunes are extant, and many more tunes are falsely attributed to him. He
began studying the harp at the age of 18 when he was blinded by smallpox. At 21
he set out with a horse, a guide, and his harp to make his way as an itinerant
harper. He was welcomed into the best houses in Ireland and was always treated
with respect and esteem. Many of his pieces are "planxties", or songs written
in honor of his patrons or members of their households. He sometimes used well-
known tunes and wrote new words for them. Only a few of his lyrics still exist.
This planxty was written in honor of George Brabazon of County Mayo, who was then
a young bachelor. The tune is known in Scotland as Twa Bonnie Maidens.

BRISKLY & BOLDLY

CAROLAN

Scarborough Fair

LEISURELY, WITH A LILT

ENGLAND

Before you begin this lesson, go back and re-read the pages about how to hold
the harp and hand position to be sure that you are playing correctly

Lesson 6

EXERCISE 6 A

EXERCISE 6 B

EXERCISE 6 C

The Grenadier and the Lady

LEISURELY & FIRMLY

ENGLAND

As you already know, a quarter note ♩ gets one beat, or two eighth notes ♫ get one beat. Sometimes three notes get one beat. This is called a <u>triplet</u> All three notes are of equal value (1/3 of a beat) and in total they <u>get one</u> beat. There is a triplet in the fourth measure of this next piece. To count this triplet measure, say "1 & 2 & 3 & 4 & uh". The "4 & uh" are the 3 notes of the triplet and are said and played a little faster than the other counts.

My Love is Like A Red, Red Rose

At the end of this piece are the Italian words DC al Fine. DC stands for "da capo"
or "from the beginning" and "al Fine" means "to the end". It means that when you
get to the "DC al Fine" you go back to the beginning and play through to where it
says "Fine" or "end". In this piece you play to the end of the written music,
start over and play through to the double bar in the 8th measure.

This is the tune that is commonly used with Robert Burns' poem of this name.

SLOWLY & TENDERLY   SCOTLAND

Searching for Lambs

This piece is in $\frac{5}{4}$ time, which means that there are 5 beats in each measure. Don't be surprised if this seems unnatural to you. It is a rare time signature for Western music. Count it very carefully as you learn it to be sure you have it right.

Also notice that the left hand changes from the bass clef to the treble clef, and then back again to the bass clef. This is done to reduce the number of ledger lines.

MODERATELY & HAUNTINGLY   BRITISH ISLES

❖❖

Both of the next two pieces are in $\frac{6}{8}$ time. That means that there are 6 beats in each measure, but that an <u>eighth</u> note (rather than a quarter note) gets one beat. Therefore, these are the time values of the notes in these pieces:

♪ = 1 beat (eighth note)

♪. = 1½ beat (dotted eighth note)

♩ = 2 beats (quarter note)

♩. = 3 beats (dotted quarter note)

There is another kind of note in these pieces: the <u>sixteenth note</u> ♬. It has two flags. It is held half as long as an eighth note, or ½ beat. Two or more sixteenth notes can be written together with two beams replacing the two flags:

42

When sixteenth notes are written with dotted
eighth notes, only part of the beam is
written next to the sixteenth note:

In these pieces, sixteenth notes are written
in one of the two following ways. The two
ways are written a bit differently, but they
mean the same thing.

count ① & 2 &③ & or ① & 2 &③ &

Greensleeves   or   What Child is This?

LEISURELY & ROMANTICALLY

ENGLAND

Planxty Irwin

The repeat signs ‖: :‖ in this piece indicate that you play section A twice and then play section B twice.

Carolan wrote this planxty for Colonel John Irwin of County Sligo, Ireland.

LEISURELY & FLOWINGLY

CAROLAN

44

Lesson 7

EXERCISE 7

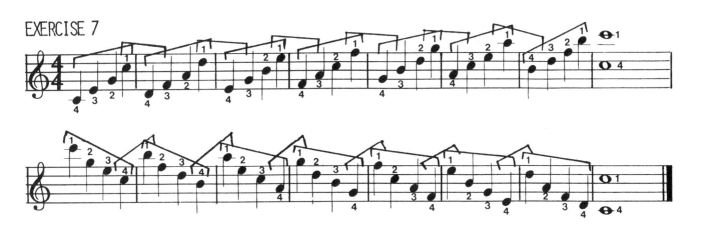

Sometimes when a section of a piece is repeated, the last measure (or several measures) is different the second time through. This ⌐1.⌐ is placed over the ending measure that is played the first time through, and this ⌐2. is placed over the measure that is played <u>instead</u> the second time. For example:

play measures 1 through 5, go back to the beginning and play 1 through 4, <u>SKIP 5</u>, and play 6 instead, continue with 7 etc.

This occurs twice in the next piece as follows:
 a. play the first half of the piece with the first ending
 b. repeat the first half of the piece with the second ending instead
 c. continue with the second half of the piece using the new first ending
 d. repeat the second half of the piece using the new second ending.

Trip To Sligo or Lark on the Strand

LEISURELY & HAPPILY

IRELAND

Minuet

MODERATELY

J. S. BACH

Farewell

SLOWLY & EMOTIONALLY

48

Lesson 8

A <u>chord</u> is two or more notes that are played at the same time. In this lesson,
two-note chords are played with one hand.

This exercise is played with one hand. Practice with the right hand and then with
the left an octave lower. Then play both hands together.

EXERCISE 8

49

The Christ Child's Lullaby

SLOWLY & TENDERLY

HEBRIDES

Cherry Blooms

St. Anthony's Chorale

MODERATELY & STATELY

JOSEPH HAYDN

52

Lesson 9

Chords of three or more notes are usually "broken". This means that rather than play all the notes together at the same time, you "break" the chord, playing the notes in <u>rapid</u> succession from the lowest note to the highest note. Do this very quickly. This is what gives the chords their characteristic "harp-like" sound. Chords are always broken from the bottom to the top, that is, from the lowest note to the highest.

EXERCISE 9 A

EXERCISE 9 B

EXERCISE **9** C

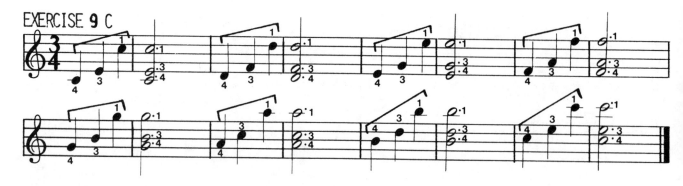

This sign 𝄐 is a _fermata_, meaning "pause" in German or Italian. This means to hold the note a bit longer than usual (or pause on it) before continuing. If you are counting the beats in the measure, stop counting at the fermata and pause before continuing to count.

Lullaby

In this piece, the melody begins in the left hand and then continues with the right. Also, notice that both hands are written in the treble clef.

LEISURELY & SWEETLY

WALES

Johnny has Gone for a Soldier

In this piece the melody, or tune, is played with the left hand.

SLOWLY & MOURNFULLY

USA

Flow Gently, Sweet Afton

The words to "Flow Gently Sweet Afton" were written by Robert Burns. This tune can also be used with "Away in a Manger".

LEISURELY & PEACEFULLY   ALEXANDER HUME - SCOTLAND

theme from the
New World Symphony

SLOWLY & STATELY

ANTON DVORAK

Lesson 10

EXERCISE 10 A

EXERCISE 10 B

EXERCISE 10 C

EXERCISE 10 D

Cockles and Mussels

LEISURELY & SIMPLY

IRELAND

59

Au Clair de la Lune

This song, written by the opera composer in the court of Louis XIV, became a popular folk song in France.

MODERATELY & SIMPLY

J. B. LULLY

Shenandoah

VERY SLOWLY & FLOWING

USA

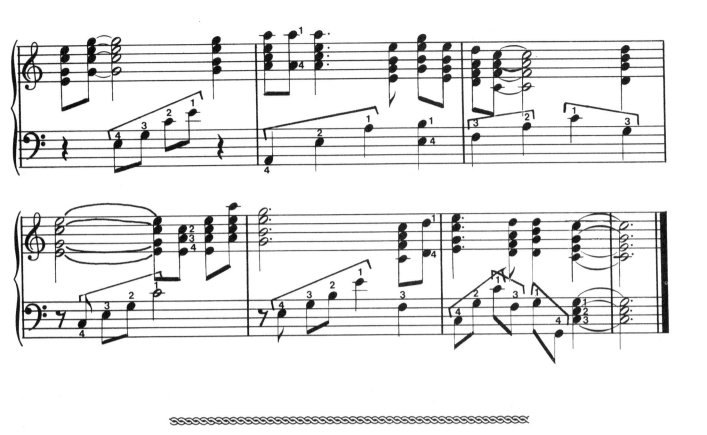

Lesson 11

When playing 5 consecutive descending notes, it is often best to <u>slide</u> the thumb from the first to the second note. This ⌢ indicates that the thumb should slide. For example, in the first measure of this exercise, place your fingers on G, E, D, C (skipping the F string). Slide your thumb across the G and F and then play the E, D, C as usual. Be sure to slide rather than pluck with your thumb. Practice this exercise until all 5 notes in each group sound even.

EXERCISE 11 A

"Cross-overs" and "cross-unders" are techniques used when playing a series of 5 or more notes that are either all ascending or all descending. These techniques are slight variations on the methods of placing discussed in the first two lessons.

Example 1: Ascending (cross-unders)

   a. place all 4 fingers on the first 4 strings (C, D, E, F)
   b. play fingers 4, 3, and 2
   c. before playing 1, bring 4 under the thumb and place it on G
   d. play the thumb
   e. pivot the hand towards you on the 4th finger so that the hand and fingers are in the proper position
   f. place 3, 2, and 1
   g. play 4, 3, 2, and 1

This can also be done by crossing the 3rd finger under, instead of the 4th, as in Exercise 11 C.

Example 2: Descending (cross-overs)

   a. place all 4 fingers on the first 4 strings (C, B, A, G)
   b. play fingers 1, 2, and 3
   c. before playing 4, bring the thumb over 4 and place it on the F
   d. play 4
   e. open the hand down from the thumb so that the fingers are in the proper position
   f. place 2, 3, and 4
   g. play 1, 2, 3, and 4

This can also be done using only three fingers (1, 2, and 3) with the thumb crossing over the 3rd finger, as in Exercise 11 C.

EXERCISE 11 B

EXERCISE 11 C

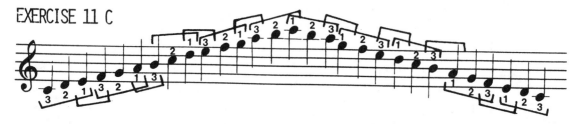

62

Gilliekrankie

This tune was probably written by a 17th Century Irish harper named Thomas Connelan who was living in Scotland. It commemorates a battle fought in Scotland in 1689.

BRISKLY & MARCH-LIKE

In these exercises, the cross-overs or cross-unders are followed by chords. The sequence is the same as in the examples before Exercise 11B, except that one finger is left out in steps f and g (i.e. the chords in Exercise D don't use the 3rd finger, and the chords in Exercise E don't use the 2nd finger).

EXERCISE 11 D

EXERCISE 11 E

When a bracket contains one or more notes followed by a chord, only one finger for the chord is placed at the beginning of the bracket. In these examples, finger 1 from the chord is placed with the finger(s) for the first note(s). The other fingers in the chord are placed right before the chord is played.

Ash Grove

LEISURELY & EMOTIONALLY

WALES

Wild Mountain Thyme

Robert Tannahill (1774-1810)., a weaver in Paisley, Scotland, wrote words to this tune.
SLOWLY & LONGINGLY

Lesson 12

A <u>glissando</u>, commonly called a "gliss" or is the best known and most easily recognizable harp effect. It is produced by sliding a finger either up or down along the strings. A gliss can be played slowly or quickly and can cover a few or many notes. Often ascending and descending glisses are played alternately, producing a wave-like effect. Ascending glisses are played with the fleshy part of finger 2. Descending ones are played with the thumb.

This ascending gliss begins on the lower C at the beginning of beat 1, and ends on the higher C at the beginning of beat 2. The length of the gliss is always the number of beats of the first note (i.e. this first note gets one beat, so the gliss itself gets that one beat).

Practice playing ascending and descending glisses with both hands (separately) at various speeds until all of the notes sound even.

❖❖❖

A <u>harmonic</u> is a method of playing a string so that it sounds an octave higher than its normal pitch. This is done by touching the string in the center so that only half of the string vibrates, and then plucking the string. The note produced has a lovely bell-like sound.

Harmonics are played differently with the right and left hands.

RIGHT HAND
Curl the fingers in towards the palm. Press the first knuckle of finger 2 against the center of the string. Keep the thumb up. Gently pluck the string with the thumb and move the hand away from the string at the same time. Don't force it.

LEFT HAND
Place the fleshy part of the side of the hand (below the little finger) against the middle of the string. The thumb should be up with the fingers relaxed, not in to the palm. Pluck the string gently with the thumb and move the hand away from the string at the same time. Don't force it.

RIGHT
HAND

LEFT (seen from the
HAND right hand side
    of the harp)
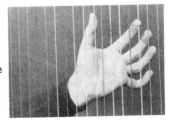

Harmonics are clear only at the center of the strings. Move your hand up and down near the center of the string until you find the spot where the harmonic is the clearest. Be sure to keep your thumb high to get the best possible harmonic.

Harmonics are written where they are played, and sound an octave higher. In other words, when reading music, play the harmonic on the string that is written, but it will produce a sound an octave higher.

Harmonics are written like this:

Practice harmonics with both hands until they are clear.

❖❖❖

Minstrel Boy

MODERATELY & MARCH-LIKE

IRELAND

Southwind

SLOWLY & BEAUTIFULLY

IRELAND

Sheebeg Sheemore

Carolan used this melody (originally called The Bonny Cuckoo) and wrote words to
it for his first composition. The lyrics told about a battle between the fairies
of Sheebeg (the Little Fairy Hill) and Sheemore (the Big Fairy Hill).

LEISURELY & LILTINGLY

Jesu, Joy of Man's Desiring

MODERATELY & EXPRESSIVELY

J. S. BACH

CONGRATULATIONS! You have now completed
this book. You're a real harper! Write
and let me know how it went, and I'll
send you information on the next book
in this series.

APPENDIX

TUNING

TUNING BASICS

1. Put the tuning key on the right side (square side) of the tuning pin for the string you are going to tune. Hold it with your right hand. Be sure the tuning key is on the correct pin, or you will tend to break strings by tightening them too much.

2. Determine the correct pitch of the string (i.e. A, B, etc.) and play that note on a pitch pipe or piano.

3. Pluck the string with your left hand. While it is still sounding, turn the tuning key until the pitch of the string matches the pitch pipe or piano. Always push the tuning key in towards the harp as you are turning it. This helps keep the tuning pins tight.

TUNING A NEW HARP

When tuning a new harp, or one that is not tuned up to pitch, always tune the lowest string first and then tune the strings consecutively all the way to the top. This allows the soundboard to adjust to the tension of the strings. After you have tuned all of the strings, start again at the bottom and repeat the whole process. This will need to be done quite a few times on a new harp before the strings stretch and adjust to their pitches. After the strings have stabilized, this won't be necessary. Once the strings are holding their pitch, you can begin to fine tune your harp.

FINE TUNING, OR EVERYDAY TUNING

1. Tune all of the strings from middle C up to the next C, following the steps in Tuning Basics above.

2. Check to see if the notes in this octave sound in tune with each other by playing the following notes: C-E-G-C, C-F-A-C, D-G-B. Each group should sound in tune. Adjust them as necessary.

3. Now tune the rest of the harp by tuning the octaves. That is, tune all of the G's to the one G that you have in tune; tune all of the F's to the F that is in tune, etc.

4. After all of the strings have been tuned in this manner, check the notes in step 2 in each octave and adjust as necessary.

5. Your harp is now ready to be played!

HARP CARE

by Christopher Caswell

The harp is a sturdy instrument, but there are stresses which will cause parts of it to act in certain ways. Knowing about these stresses will enable you to care for your harp properly.

The tension of the strings is constantly trying to pull the harmonic curve to one side. This also tries to twist the pillar in the same direction. Two parts of the harp help counter this tension. Most harps have a metal plate over the pillar/curve joint to keep it from fracturing. Harps also have either a laminated pillar, or a cross-piece called a "T" to keep the pillar straight. If either of these parts show stress, consult a harp maker.

Soundboards will naturally pull up in the center. It is when this "arch" occurs that a harp gets its mature voice. Other things happen at this time as well. A slight shifting will occur where the soundboard meets the box. Small cracks may open at the top or bottom of the soundboard. Neither of these things are cause for alarm, as long as they don't get too large. A small crack in the soundboard may even improve the sound a bit.

Strings will break occasionally in the natural course of events. If a lot break repeatedly, make sure they are not too heavy. If a few break repeatedly in the same place, check for any rough places or sharp edges which might contact the string. If a string won't stay in tune, make sure the tuning pin is tight. If it isn't, place your tuning key on the tuning pin and push it in toward the harp until the tuning pin grips well. If the string still won't stay tuned, make sure the knot isn't slipping.

In General:

Don't leave your harp exposed to sunlight or spotlights for too long. Sunlight through a closed window is especially bad.

Keep your harp from long exposure to very dry environments. Unless the harp was made in an arid place, it may crack.

Keep your harp protected from rapid and/or extreme temperature changes as much as possible. An insulated or padded case will help a lot.

Never tighten the strings much above the note for which they were intended. Never string a harp with overly heavy strings. Soundboard damage could occur in both cases.

When traveling with your harp by air, always lower the pitch by a couple of notes. The cargo holds of most passenger planes are pressurized, but aren't always protected from heat and cold. When shipping your harp on a non-passenger plane, take all tension off the strings.

Don't put anything on the harp that may damage the finish or weaken the glue joints.

Remember: when tuning up (as in a new harp), go from the long string to the short; when tuning down (as when shipping), go from the short to the long.

That's about it. It's mostly common sense.

REPLACING NYLON or GUT STRINGS

1. Remove the broken string from the tuning pin and pull it down through the hole in the string rib and out through a sound hole.

2. Select the proper string to replace the broken one.

3. Some strings have stops built into them: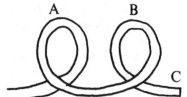

   All other strings need to be knotted so that the end won't pull through the hole in the string rib when tightened.

   a. Make two loops (A & B) near the end (C) of the string.

   b. Insert loop B through loop A from back to front.

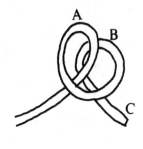
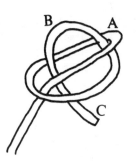
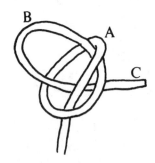

   c. For extra strength, insert a piece of another string or a headless nail through loop A.

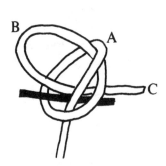

   d. Pull loop A tight around loop B.

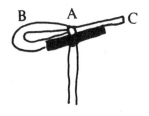

4. Insert the other end of the string (i.e. the end that is not tied) from the inside of the soundbox up through the hole in the string rib. Pull the string through until it is stopped by the knot.

Steps 3 and 4 can be done in the opposite order by pushing the string through the hole in the string rib from the top, then tying the knot, then pulling the string back up until it is stopped by the knot.

5. Thread the string through the hole in the tuning pin. Leave it a bit slack. It should be able to wrap around the tuning pin at least twice before it is tight.

6. Place the string in the groove of the bridge pin. If your harp has sharping levers, be sure the string is in the correct position in relation to them.

7. Hold the end of the string flat against the tuning pin with your left hand. With your right hand, place the tuning key on the tuning pin and turn it away from you one complete turn. This will lock the end of the string in place so it won't slip.

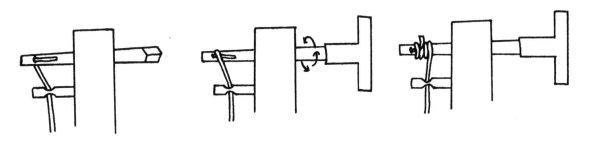

8. Slowly continue turning the key until the string is up to the proper pitch.

9. The string will not hold its pitch very well until it has stretched a bit. Therefore, you will have to tune it frequently for several days until it has adjusted to its pitch.

10. You should trim off any excess string about ½ inch from the tuning pin. If your strings are wrapped strings, that is, one piece of strings wrapped around another (looking like this ⟟⟟⟟⟟⟟), do not cut these strings. If you do, they will unwind.

Note: If the color wears off the red and blue strings, you can re-color them with permanent ink magic markers.

REPLACING METAL STRINGS

You will need a pair of snub-nosed pliers to change metal strings.

1. Remove the broken string from the tuning pin and pull it down through the hole in the string rib and out through a sound hole. Be sure to save the toggle (the metal piece that the string is wrapped around) if there is one.

2. Select the proper string to replace the broken one.

3. Insert the end of the string through the hole in the string rib and out through a sound hole.

4. a. For heavier strings: fold the string around the toggle about 2 inches from the end of the string.

b. For lighter strings: bend about 3 inches of the string back against itself. Place the toggle in the center of this doubled section and fold the string over the toggle.

5. Wrap the string tightly around the main part of the string 5 or 6 times.

6. Pull the string up until it is stopped by the toggle. If the wrapping shows above the string rib, re-do step 4, folding over a shorter amount of the string, or wrap it closer in step 5.

7. Cut the string about 3 inches above the tuning pin.

8. Thread the string through the hole in the tuning pin. Put it through twice for the lighter strings. Make a sharp bend in the end of the string.

9. With your right hand, place the tuning key on the tuning pin. Turn the key away from you to tighten the string. Guide the string with your left hand so that it winds properly on the tuning pin.

10. When the string is up to pitch, be sure that it is in line with the others and that the last wind is not touching the wood or any of the other winds on the tuning pin.

11. Until the string stretches completely, you will need to tune it often.

12. Color the C's red or the F's blue with a permanent ink magic marker.

SHARPING LEVERS

Most nylon-strung or gut-strung harps are equipped with sharping levers. These are levers that are right below the bridge pins. When turned sideways or flipped up (depending on the model) they shorten the length of the string, thereby raising the pitch. This higher pitch is called a <u>sharp</u> ♯ . For example, the note produced by an F string with the sharping lever in contact with it is called F sharp (F♯); a C string becomes a C♯, etc.

In written music, the sharp sign will be written <u>in front of the note</u> to be sharped.   F♯ =

Sometimes sharp signs are written at the beginning of a piece:

 indicates that all F's in the piece are to be sharped. To play this piece, set the levers on all the F's before you begin to play.

 indicates that all F's and C's are to be sharped. Set the F and C levers before you begin to play.

TEACH YOURSELF TO PLAY THE FOLK HARP VIDEO

TEACH YOURSELF TO PLAY
THE FOLK HARP VIDEO

by SYLVIA WOODS

This video is a companion to Sylvia Woods' best-selling harp book TEACH YOURSELF TO PLAY THE FOLK HARP which has been used by thousands of harp players and teachers all over the world. In this informative video, Sylvia Woods gives helpful hints and instruction as she plays through the pieces in the 12 lessons of the book. This is an excellent way to see "how it should be done", and receive helpful advice from Sylvia. This video is 1 hour and 40 minutes long.

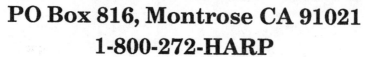

SYLVIA WOODS HARP CENTER
PO Box 816, Montrose CA 91021
1-800-272-HARP

**Write or call the Sylvia Woods Harp Center for a
FREE Mail Order Catalog
which includes over 50 folk harp music books,
over 100 harp cassettes & CDs by a variety of harp players,
harp gift items, harp accessories,
and exellent high quality harps.**

OTHER BOOKS BY SYLVIA WOODS

**Pachelbel's Canon
The Harp Of Brandiswhiere
Irish Dance Tunes For All Harps
40 O'Carolan Tunes For All Harps
Andrew Lloyd Webber Arranged For Harp
Music Theory & Arranging Techniques For Folk Harps
Hymns And Wedding Music For All Harps
50 Christmas Carols For All Harps
Chanukah Music For All Harps
Songs Of The Harp**

RECORDINGS BY SYLVIA WOODS

**The Harp of Brandiswhiere
Three Harps for Christmas, Volume 1
Three Harps for Christmas, Volume 2**

You can order these books and recordings from your local music store,
or directly from the Sylvia Woods Harp Center.

TABLE OF SYMBOLS

ALPHABETICAL INDEX OF TUNES